MESSAGE

To Katharine
Happy 50th!
Love, Pook

MESSAGE

POEMS BY

Paula Bonnell

MillCreek Press

Boston

Vancouver

ACKNOWLEDGMENTS

Some of the poems in this book have appeared (one in
another version) in *Blue Unicorn, The Fiddlehead, floating
island, Gryphon, The Pawn Review,* and *Poet Lore.* "Midwest,"
which first appeared in *Blue Unicorn,* was included in the
*ANTHOLOGY OF MAGAZINE VERSE & YEARBOOK OF
AMERICAN POETRY,* 1986-1988 edition.

"Forsythia" was first published in the Andrew Mountain
Press's *A Poem in a Pamphlet* series. "Dream Phrase" was
projected on the underside of an airplane at the Cambridge
River Festival as part of the Imaginary Press's *Star Poems III.*

Library of Congress Cataloging-in-Publication Data
Bonnell, Paula
Message: poems/by Paula Bonnell
p.   cm.
ISBN 1-928668-04-6 (acid-free paper)
I. Title
PS   1999

CIP

Published by

MillCreek Press
Suite 840
50 Congress Street
Boston, Massachusetts
&
Vancouver, British Columbia
Canada

CONTENTS

MESSAGE

A CONTINUAL GOODBYE

EURYDICE

MESSAGE

MESSAGE

Start out down by the Golden Nugget and Hogan's fruit stand,
both somewhere past Hillje's,
and take the road west into your art
into a real Texas free of symbols,
distinctive as turnips, slick as butter, bruisable as flesh.
In fact, it is flesh
after the coating of nuggets and daggers
is boiled off by the sun
and you are down to
nougaty weather and dust.

If you can spare it, spit
to rid your mouth of rusted expectations.
Then squint until the details come naturally:
white horses stolid in the tomato patch down by the bridge.
Each is grey as the weathered wood
of the bridge planks or the tomato stakes.

There are fields of fervent grass level as water
and a few snags in the river when you
get past Goliad.
Stop in the field where heavy-wristed trees
reach solicitously to their shadows
and grass as deep as the first burl bows with the heat.

THE GENIUS OF CHILDHOOD

The prodigies of its weather are theatrical from the first.
There is an orchestra of black shapes,
a silence before the overture.
The set is curtainless.
On the backdrop a funiculus
dangles from the clouds into the glowering dank below.
A tumid hush is stuffed under the trees.

The white palms of the leaves
wag nervously
as the torpor of the air is ruptured.
Initially, a stingy nattering,
then its substitute: a wash of pizzicati.
This stutters to a stinging scat singing;
this hoarsens to a thousand rude glissandos of rain.

A white shock shows how big the stage is
and how exposed the cast.
Which ones are the extras? which the audience?
The storm blurs such nice distinctions.
It drenches us in a wet participation,
full of the cold of fear, and something else.
This is a ceremony we perform.

The trees do their complex dance of obeisance.
The seeing stops.
There is clamor and slamming,
a hundred obscure thunders.
All is lost in the glossolalia we utter,
the convulsions of the trees;
we inhale the terrific rapture of the wind.

FORSYTHIA

In March my mother would force the forsythia
bringing them in from the melting yard
and in the warmth of the house
flowers would flow from the freckled wands
to make ours a springhouse
sure with the force of forsythia
ballooning a silk of sky unsnowing above us.

The drifts of the sky today fall to
dissolve in horizony heat on the tip
of the highway which lunges toward our car.
Its spots swell to become lumps of rusty fur
and it shoots out behind us so fast
that the fur fluffs in the haze
and the skunk smell speeds away

to be lost in the rushes of distance
where our yard of forsythia
blooms. The bushes there are
foolish with yellow — their long arms
dangle and wag at the hummocks
of crabgrass, their roots
anchor in the mound where
Mrs. Greiner's dog was buried in 1942.

PRYING OPEN *DEMAND*

Script for an Animated Cartoon

I dreamed it:
the *d* cracked off
with a chisel.
Deman — a kind of demon
to take it away from him.

Unstapling — the *e* emerges,
bending him out of shape
to be *D'man* —
burly, fat folding his face,
eyeless as a nightstick.

Then damned
if the apostrophe didn't split off the *D*,
falling away with it.
Man, stock still now,
thrusts out of the packings.

Off with the *n!*
This is it —
the dread androgyny sets in,
like a quick-growing womb.
The swollen *M*, the little *a* of strain
deliver the *n*. *Ma!* that felt odd.
This is really the end!

But no; there's more —
the *M* melts,
and look — there's not a thing
godlike about it after all.
Under the table,
the letters have *mend'd* themselves;
the anonymous, universal *a* curls up in the gap.
Men - dad — be one with us.

DRAUGHT

Saturday morning sleep is like the froth in a beerglass —
a head of dreams on the long pour of night.

JANUARY SEMBLANCES

Houston, 1973

Just before the reputed end of the war,
snow came for a visit;
elegiac as somebody's old childhood
    stuffed away in a closet.

It had the imaginary yet substantial quality
    of mothballs.
When we shook it out it was
snowman stuff all right,
mittful after mittful of it.

By mid-afternoon the population doubled:
on lawns
simples, caricatures, ideals, myth men,
muffled ones, Schmoos, and a snow hermaphrodite
appeared, incredible as peace.

IT is like being a cat:
First, to be called,
then to be stroked,
then to rub back with the fur
and to arch,
then to begin the thrumming inside
And suddenly like a cat to leap —
till the floor whirls about and lifts
to arrive at the feet;
Then, self-satisfied, like a cat,
to curl up and sleep.

WHAT JAMIE SAID

Your palm goes limp — it has soft innards.
It gasps like a lung,
clasping my hand with a pulmonary beat
just as you submerge in sleep.

We are husks, we are shells,
gulping our palpable dreams,
going down like clams in the shallows
to settle in the mud of the id —
its pulsing whispers, its greenbrown heat.

Here in the gleaming fluid of this sea,
you resuscitate me.
I balloon up to you,
trembly as allsex, warmly blundering,
expansive to the cusp.
The hinge grasps everything,
releasing a few signal bubbles.

POETRY

It comes on like a seizure
set off by the deadly morse bursting between
trees or railroad station pillars.
The shock of recognition
knocks you into yourself
and you must haul yourself out
or you'll come to
choking on your tongue.

ANAESTHESIA

The perfect artist is a machine
to produce the unexpected
from the quotidian. The finished product is
same enough so you know it,
rank enough so it hurts.
It reeks with a diagnostic smell.

Amid the metallic details of the hospital
you are the patient, waiting, waiting
for the cut.
You are sexless as a refrigerated flower.

The air goes glaucous.

The incision blurts the clangor of change.

Without compunction the florist renounces you;
it is said you have healed.

The surgeon abandons you,
filing away your chart with its curious protuberances.
(It later plays a bit part in his text.)
What you nourished — its calcium "teeth," its "hair" —
is given to the students. It will endure like the truth.

MIDWEST

My heart is like Chicago's Union Station.
Once it was full of a thunder of arrivals, departures.
In the gusty ostentation of its spaces blinked
    tremulous Rebeccas, fresh as eggs from the farm;
and the pull of the trains boomed in its aortal vaults.
How the hicks hobnobbed, then shushed in the din,
    eyeing the moguls eye
      those pigtails wobbling in the holes in straw hats!
It was big, big enough to contain the city.

Now it is filled with commuter regularities —
the lisping of papers,
      the oblong rumbles,
          the routine comings & goings.
In the club cars,
      under tables of bridge games,
          bobble the briefcases
       with their inbound sandwiches
      and their outbound stock quotes.
Cards coded with tiny symbols cover each other;
      the queen falls to the ace.
Back in the station the benches are glossy with waiting.
The place is written up in the guidebooks,
      a must for the ruddy tourists.
It is part of Chicago, this pump, this station, this heart.

HEALING

There is no red season, only blue, green, yellow, and brown
until the wound opens and
you are gone.
Gravity is shaken out of you
onto the ground.
Then you must walk on it.

Into the tunnel with you. Into and into it.
It is interior only; you have lost the entrance.
It has no end.

Outside
there is no blood season, only crisp, tender, bright, and full,
but you are inside,
you are caught in the flood.
This is the blood season

till it dries to black
and you are left to bleach out
tear your hands, hair, and legs out
out of the scab
till you can walk and cry and sing.
You say
there is no red season, only white, yellow, green, and gold.

INTRUSIONS – 4 a.m.

The thwacking of newspapers on the stoops;
the shaking of shadows on the blind.
The roses scrape their thorns on the shutters.
In one apartment the bedsprings creak
to be heard in another.
Breathlessness — unventilated heat.

Oblique rain hits the screen.
The projectionist shows a dream:
in the choir, there is a scuffle.
Emerging from the robes, a puffball angel
drifts like a dandelion over the chancel
empurpled by light from the rose window.

The center of the rose expands kaleidoscopically,
ceaselessly. Slow motion sequences . . .
zoom shots . . . farrago of techniques.
The emulsion melts.

QUOTIDIAN, DATELINE MANHATTAN

Garbage-can-lid alarm.

Poked by the toast,
the soft-boiled eggs spill their guts.

Last night's lovers shift their haunches
in terry-cloth robes on canebottom chairs.

The pigeons push off from the fire escape.
Garbage-can lids settle in.

Belt buckle, key chain; police whistle, newspapers;
change rattles in pockets and it's off, off, office again.

early evening

The birds fall from the trees like leaves,
and the cats, resting up from resting up, take their ease,
taking in birds as eyes' appetizers to the night's hunt.
Silence and balance tremble in a troubling breeze.
Umber spreads till the sky is a spinnaker —
and it begins:
the rushing of violence between the cats and the birds,
the lashing of branches as the fat go fleet with their skillful
falling that outdoes flight
till the light bleeds a little onto the sheet.
Then, laving the tufts and the dark globules of the trees,
comes the lift and the light volubility of the birds.

Mouse your heart
announces beats
measures without
logic or magic
nibbles the lease

Quibble the count
leisureless mouse

Mouse you sound
closure to feast
suffer to speak
clangor not hunger
clapbeat love deathmeat sweet

WORDSWORTH

graduated without honors;
Hart Crane's father
invented Lifesavers
and Wallace Stevens's wife
modeled for the Liberty-head dime.

You were afraid
that's all we'd remember
from your classes —
that and the birds.
You'd been talking
of Shelley's skylark,
Keats's nightingale
and Yeats's swan.
"All those poets
really wanted to be birds,"
you said.

And a Vietnam vet
in the back of the room
who'd never said a
word before
stopped you.
"Could you repeat that
please?"
"I said, 'All those poets
really wanted to be birds,' "
you said.

"That's what I thought
you said,"
he said,
and got up
and walked out.

That left the
rest of us
alone with your
voice reading
Emily Dickinson
and Walt Whitman
so blue and so green
that I still hear you
on every page.

IMPOSSIBLE NECESSARY SAINT

There is a saint patient as a machine
alone on a cloud seen by a novice
who, asked to submit three choices for her name,
writes on a page, "St. Jude, St. Jude, St. Jude"

There is a perfect Antarctica
where Gould sees behind a scrim of snow
a penguin. He calls "Snowman! Scholar!"

PARTICULARS

Light off the sea
assaults the resort windows.
The couple like children in the bed
soothes each other.
Ululations — the loosening, the waves;
waves subsiding. Ellipsis.

To wash, to dress.
Flesh of a poached egg glistens.
In the porch shadows, a summer of voices.
In the sun, a glare of silence to wade.

Vendors; babble; flies.
Spreading a towel,
eating a waffle.
The waves tump on the beach.
Sun oil spills on the sand.
Bright garments, sunflush.
Savor of salt water, horseplay.
Washing ashore.

The grit of going back — lugging the stuff.
Ablutions — double rinse.
Dinner amid wicker —
salad specificity,
broiled chicken with basil, with garlic;
rice and nuts.
Whisper of rockers, of fans.
Hands touch.
The sea swallows the sun.

THE OFFICE

We have all lost our cushy staff jobs,
our offices with windows,
we who were consorts to figures,
escorts to words. We have had to become
mothers and fathers to departments
full of brats and budgets
and problems no one admits.

As usual
it is all decisions
with diagrams drawn afterwards.
It is phones and questions.
It is doings undone,
and a good thing
there are no windows.
Our paychecks are punctuation now,
not prospects, and it's just
a little quieter after five o'clock.

HAPPINESS IS AN UNENDING BOLIVIA

The cypress survives the salt water;
La Paz continues; everything does.

The death of particular flowers is hardly noticeable.
They will cover you up before you begin to stink.

THE DISPOSSESSION OF FROGS

Sunday night.
Settled in the grass of the vacant lot,
frogs are chewing on Cs and Ks.
(Tomorrow construction will start.)

Wind and thrumming, a full moon.
In his dreams, the seller cartoons:
rubber skins ballooning with profits.
(The bulldozer snores on a full tank.)

Now there is a recess of frog noise.
The dew blooms with small lights.
(Monday coffee, thermoses, workmen.)

Now it is eight: they are dozing the pond.

Now it is five: they have leveled the lot.

Bales of wire are pitched at the edge of the site
to be embedded in Tuesday's slab.

A hundred yards beyond the debris,
by the purple flowers and the beer bottle shards,
frogs ready their throats for tonight
in the ditch by the railroad tracks.

TRAVELING EAST

I thought of stopping to take a photograph. I would call it
"Mist and the Ravages of Tent Caterpillars."
But the mirror on my 35 was jammed,
and this was interstate — EMERGENCY STOPPING ONLY —
just a few trucks and tourists cocooned on the shoulder;
so I held the truck to 50 on the grade,
watching the yellows and whites converge
to blank out objects, distinctions, horizon.
It was all one.
I entered it on a lizard-tongue of a road.

Across the median, three tractor-trailer rigs
wormed their way up the concrete.
Ahead a punchhole of a sun bit through the murk,
and off to the sides small glosses shone
where caterpillars made their cotton candy of the trees.
I am like them:
coming out of the nurturing country
into expectations disparate as leaves,
I make mouthings of trucks, fog, worms,
and bundle the landscape with my states of mind.

A CONTINUAL GOODBYE

Shouts, yells cloud the air with sound
Rhythmic calls of blue! are screamed beside
Us yelling red, red —
Silence-cleared air, whistle-pierced
Holds the gym in suspension.
In the scramble for the rebound
A charging player careens toward our bench.
His hands thwack the wall behind me
But before he bounds away
I feel a hot pressure on my mouth
Bitter salty lips pushed on mine.
Then the strange boy is gone
A stain of blue left on my red uniform sweater.

Riding home through the darkness
I see the cornfields, desolate,
Pass the window.
Where is the sweetness?

CHANCETREE

Comes Chancetree
Lost in dim mist
Broom trunk stands aslant
Light brims over cold clouds
Chancetree starts and looms
Winds flow
    Then
Cliffedge soaks up the sun
Leaves' skill seizes the light
Brews sap rushing upbark
    And
Roots rive and slope
Clouds lid updrafts
Sun blisters in the high skin
    Wait . . .
The silent light tide moves

    Soon
Chancetree flings its shadow east
Leaves clatter in air currents
Grass mutters in undertows
Trance seeps in
    Then
Chancetree lives
In the day past

DREAM PHRASE

Apple, pineapple, rainbow-dried

LUD

The young man crossed the road,
    slowed, stood with one foot just inside
    the shadow puddled on the walkway.
    Lud's mound of flesh, molded in uncertain shapes,
    shed clumps of limb, hip over his chair.
    His hands slumped like downed blimps in his lap.
    Lud: in each cheek an army of bristles camped;
    the wet marbles of his eyes wobbled under flabby lids.
The young man beckoned, jerking his head toward the road.
    But with eyelids slackened and a deliberate tremor of his jaw,
    Lud spat, refused, and sat, inhabiting his body,
    lugubrious in the sun.

Possessions not mine — things by another held
charm with a borrowed spell, spell pseudonyms
I read with curiosity, finding things owned
draw me as would their owners, suggest
flesh, spirit, smile in usual stone or wood,
explain his smell in fibers not his own.
These grooves — strange paths by well-known fingers worn —
admit a presence of one gone. Here
mingled seem two selves: These things,
still things, move in manners not their own.

ONCE

He was too warm and red — like the sun
heavy as words, hot and ponderous;
he burnt the grass tresses of her hair.
When she stood in the still vibrant pool,
    the circle of his girth,
his dry breathing separated the cool layers
    of her skin, thin as india paper,
stirred and kindled her in a birth of awareness
until the wheyed skin under her glass nails sizzled.
She faced his ruddy skin, his searching eyes
He scorched her and forced her
    to face clicking facts.

His approach
    to her girdled in pallor and silk, creamy and hesitant,
made her fade and turn away.
She shuddered and prayed in his radiation
his redness glowed and yearned
    to understand, to learn her stern gentility,
    to live in her green glass eyes.
But his rays had not yet reached
    the undersides of her pebble-blind breasts
    spooned out beneath cloud-cobbled skies.
He had not touched the tender white belly of her soul.
She sighed and fled, melting into the grey light, the dew.

The scotch was bitter
the night I dreamt about luggage
Somebody else's wife, Somebody else's husband
slept in the next room
and somehow things were exceedingly grim —
I felt each thing in the living room
possessed between them
ashtrays, rag rug, creaky floors, aquarium fish.
All that was mine was
the sheer yellow nightgown
I had shoplifted that afternoon.
All things are a continual goodbye . . . .

EURYDICE

EURYDICE

i

Here comes Orpheus, thudding and pouring,
like a white fist to his first wife — that's me —
crawling between my muscles and going strong.
Ring, gongs; sing, song; we've done it again.
Rib rhythms repeat what mouth rhymes began.
. . . Lapse into sleep; I dream of another man
with eyes and questions and laughter
and gut-ease that makes me feel at home.
I stir, but before I surface, Orpheus snores
and I am lulled, settle in the down,
drowse to the blues beat of blood dreams —
nuzzling crowds and the populous circus of the night —
which I will tell him about safely in the morning
and he'll sing it out loudly in the eve.

ii

Your art was public as a phallus
mine as dark as a hole, but
all your art came from me, you bastard —
I say bastard because you had no father.
I mothered you entirely
heaving daily, nightly for your vaunted heaven.
It's all one, you know, my work and your play;
I made the pedestal you put me on
from the household dirt and my own moistures.
Made it moreover to your design.
It may kill me to get up on it,
yet you say I must be silent as I do so.
All right, give me a hand, I'll take the step.
But watch out for that lamp cord, it's

iii

Transformations are my business
but you will not get me out of my latest one.
Come into my mirror — I am no smooth
surface now in your heats and rages —
Will it stay fluid for you to re-emerge
or like a nightmare whorehouse lock on you,
boldly thrashing? Like rich relations
the seasons announce my names: Medea,
Seda, Jasmine, Eurydice; come to
my coolnesses, the slick of my tunnels —
do not be too definite; there are no
maps to dunes or oases; sink in the
glistening grains of magic silica.
They will fuse to a glass soon enough.

iv

Perfidy, Orpheus. You were as perfidious as an orchid
showy as the phallic bloom, air-thriver,
dangler. I was the dark room you grew in.
You got so big I had to expel you,
breach as you'd be. We were both as
inevitable as flowers, breathing
and flowing to doom. Down a stairwell,
dark as a tomb, go the tendrils to
emerge in the light. You boast of dying —
I have done it and it's only
another kind of yielding, verging on
enormity, a going down, going dark, calling
and yawning, choking and snoring — blood breath —
no glory — no time — not yet — not me — knot.

v

I live like a plant on water and air
down in the earth. Leave, leopard, I have
no meat for you; I am a ruddy Venus.
If you got what you want, you'd open your
closet to an old broom, a night sponge,
a morning glory, anything but a woman.
Yet you insist on coming into my darkness.
Listen and you will hear what my silence says.
I am ready, ready for the flies on your coat;
I will remove the annoyances until you are mine.
Your growl will gurgle; I will fold my leaves
glut-sickened by sucking lies. Don't you see that
we are in peril? We are two left halves
that will lock and never get right.

vi

It was a practical suggestion she made
not to look back. Your broad back
plugged the passage, kept it dark.
As we kept going, I felt changes.
My hands were heavy, sharp, wet.
One leg dragged, my back bent.
It got harder to sing, I could only breathe;
I followed your melody in the dark.
You turned and the light leaked past your shoulders.
I saw what was the matter —
My left hand was a dish, my fingers were needles,
I was sopping and rusting, whirring and clicking.
I'll have to go back — I can't be a machine —
Orpheus, goodbye.

Orpheus, I was reared on our story;
then I lived into it. Lover, husband, affair —
magic mysteriously receded —
image to you, you to unity, unity to snake —
She has the truth. When she bit me I knew;
growth is within; out of a whole, love proceeds.
I was a hole for venom — no self — a clinger to
vainglory, phenomena; chopped in time.
I have eaten her whitenesses — I speak the truth.
We have walked her entrails; O snakeworld,
this lateknower is a vine that crawls to ground,
electric with reality. I send my sisters,
Orpheus; you will know as you separate.
Morpheus, we linger in your stores.

Let me reveal a few intimate details:
Orpheus had red hair, wore suspenders.
As a child he had an ant farm, carried an aluminum 45.
I strung beads. As a kid
I discovered a river way down under the woods.
There was no dirt
until the episode I described
yet somehow it all fit that
we wound up in a myth.
Our ordinariness is a myth
our figures cautionary yellow fingers in your brain.
Filch from us pigment for your plans —
Bleed our ochre into your outline —
Your own sun will show the art of your life.

ix

The troughs of the top are being roughed out;
the troughs of the bottom are fairly certain.
Fish flee as dead-gas-powered corpses
rise corklike through thicknesses
of the lugubrious sea. The lead one's
aqua-lunged, flipper-footed, eye-goggled.
Dragging behind is the leaden other:
dive-suited, bell-headed, grey-bodied.
How curiously animate they become
under the influence of the currents
and the melted-butter light, dripping down.
One breaks the surface and gives a lifelike shout
at the odd concavity of it all; the top falls,
unsuiting the partner. Mother! The sharks will follow.

x

We hit the bends coming up; head-bumping,
blood-booming, wave-thumping bends.
Our ears rang through the divesuit highs that were
keener than distant limbs or far-off laughter.
The laughs unreeled, peal by purple peal,
into awful grapes, like adenoids, but closer.
We were as remote from depths or waves
as barnacles on a hull, but briefly.
That didn't last. You came up first
or thought you did; I was at your feet.
That was the trough. The top doomed.
I heard echoes, heard nothing.
This is abandonment:
I am unsuited to the many-salted sea.

xi

In a question of how far we could go
we got to the mouth of open night
with the remote pandemonium of its stars
an icy jazz. Shudder of harmony —
the grass a gaff of blue. Stone enclosure.
The walls gone green as old meat;
and I acknowledge leftover angers.
The breeze mentions nothings as somethings,
and though the willow nestles her leaves
among her numerous arms (half-rustle, half-click),
coldness squeezes my ribs. Gauze
goes between us; twigs crack under
prowling feet — I recognize these riffs,
and the commotion of music unwinds to strains.

xii

The Maenads are mad with sense
ready for an outright doom, ready to damn.
Simmerers, they've boiled to a foam.
Now they'll give as good as they got
and all of it red. They're glad you're going to die.
I'm not, though I'm no kin of yours.
It's not that I'm any better than they —
no, I'm their kind all right — it's just that
I'm not ready for you again — throbber, shudderer, self-seer.
I can't feed your importance now —
I'm in some ferment of my own.
Call me former-familiar, ex-wife, suicide, what-have-you —
but let me alone for a change
I've begun a new brew and it's still too bitter to taste.

xiii

Out of brick-hearted morning,
into the soporific quiet, flooded with dreams,
flowing between rocks and crevices,
I come to the subterranean, my territory.
Your brilliance is not alight in this cave.
Only a token of your fire is in me.
I am absorbed now, not in the salt and smack of love,
but in poetry, retrospective lines.
This is a homeland: maps and compass are dross.
Each turning sings; the whole is matchless harmony.
This is the homeland: though I never knew it before —
I'd never been here but now am utterly earthen —
I cannot bring my wits to bear, I no longer
breathe your air. I have done, brothers & sisters.
Lover & mother no more; I am the one. Unearth me.

NOTES

"Grey" means blue-grey. "Gray" means yellow-gray.

Although relineation of "Midwest" was necessary to fit the format of this book, the lineation which appears in the 1986-1988 edition of the *ANTHOLOGY OF MAGAZINE VERSE & YEARBOOK OF AMERICAN POETRY* remains the definitive lineation for this poem.

"Wordsworth" honors the teaching of Don Harrell at the University of Houston.

MillCreek Press is a small press publishing fiction, poetry, criticism, fine arts, and children's books.

The text of this book is set in Century Schoolbook.